WORDS TO LIVE BY

WORDS TO LIVE BY

Quotes and Stories that Inspire our Time on Earth

DEAN GUALCO

WORDS TO LIVE BY
QUOTES AND STORIES THAT INSPIRE OUR TIME ON EARTH

iUniverse books may be ordered through booksellers or by contacting:

iUniverse
1663 Liberty Drive
Bloomington, IN 47403
www.iuniverse.com
1-800-Authors (1-800-288-4677)

Because of the dynamic nature of the Internet, any web addresses or links contained in this book may have changed since publication and may no longer be valid. The views expressed in this work are solely those of the author and do not necessarily reflect the views of the publisher, and the publisher hereby disclaims any responsibility for them.

Any people depicted in stock imagery provided by Thinkstock are models, and such images are being used for illustrative purposes only.
Certain stock imagery © Thinkstock.

ISBN: 978-1-4917-7573-8 (sc)
ISBN: 978-1-4917-7571-4 (hc)
ISBN: 978-1-4917-7572-1 (e)

Library of Congress Control Number: 2015913914

Print information available on the last page.

iUniverse rev. date: 08/27/2015

Books by Dean Gualco

What Happened to the American Dream (1995)

The Meaning of Life (2005)

The Great People of our Time (2008)

The Good Manager: A
A Guide to the 21ˢᵗ Century Manager (2010)

The Choices and Consequences of our Age:
The Disintegrating Political, Economics and Societal
Institutions of the United States (2012)

Making a Difference:
Changing the World in which you Live (2013)

To my children, Gunner and Tori,

who have given me a blessed life.

"always look for the good along the road of life"

ACKNOWLEDGMENTS

I have long believed that if you can dream the impossible dream, be determined to achieve it, never fear failure or what other people think, work hard, do what's right, and always look for the good, then you will have greatness within your grasp. Fame and fortune are not the determining factors of a great life, but rather that you fought the good fight, that you did the best you could with what you had, that you did what is right and that, in some small way, you make a difference. It has been a great ride, and for that I have been blessed, and I am thankful to many who have helped me along my path in life. Some of those people are:

- o "The Man Upstairs," who has made this all possible.
- o To mom and dad…the best that could ever be said about someone's parents is that they were "decent and honorable" people, and you far exceed that bar!
- o My maternal grandmother (Vee McCoy), and paternal grandparents (Bocci and Rose Gualco), who gave me a great reputation to live up to.
- o Bill Munroe. Find a friend like Bill and you will be set for life. I have been lucky!
- o Keith Williams. Once or twice you make a friend that lasts a lifetime.
- o Jeff Thompson. A good man who sets a great example for his children. Thanks for the inspirational contributions to this book!
- o Nick Ponticello, really one of the greatest people I have met.

- o Sierra and Shana Brucia – we have such few good friends in life, and thanks for being two of the few for me!
- o Finally, to Jon Smith. I knew Jon from the second grade until the freshman year of college, when he was killed by a drunk driver. He was just one of the best guys you will ever, ever meet. He never had the chance to live his life, to reach his destiny, to achieve greatness. Jon died more than 30 years ago, and while his chance to make a difference was short-lived this fact haunts me to make a difference with whatever time I have been granted on this Earth.

THIS BOOK

This book comprises the philosophies, quotes, lists, and stories that have influenced my life. Whether the journeys traveled to the highest mountains or to the lowest valleys, these philosophies have inspired me to never give in and never give up on that which is my destiny. These lists have served as the strategies and playbooks to guide my actions at home and at work. Finally, these stories have reminded me that no matter the victory or loss, greatness is within my grasp if I work hard and do the right thing.

My profound hope is that the philosophies and stories that have influenced my life will inspire you to create the philosophies and stories that will influence your own. Live your own life, not mine, but create the philosophies and lists that will serve as the roadmap for your journey, and the inspiration for when the light flickers along that path. Time is fleeting and boulders impede nearly every road you travel, but for those that can conquer their insecurities, overcome their burdens, do what is right, and live a decent and honorable life, the possibilities are limitless. You may not write the great American novel or shape the history that will define your generation, but you will surely live a life of excitement and adventure, and along the way – in some small way – make a difference in the world in which you lived.

If this book inspires just one person to journey along that path, I am eternally grateful.

Failure is often the consequence of daring to touch the stars,

but on those few occasions when the stars are touched
the world brightens from their luster

CONTENTS

Section 1

THE PHILOSOPHY

THE PHILOSOPHY

We spend an eternity searching for who we are, what we believe in, and how we should live our life. We devote years searching for where we should go and how we should get there. And we expend our energies searching for meaning in our time on Earth, hoping to amount to more than simply being an inhabitant and instead be someone who made a difference and helped change the course of history. Grand ambitions, to be sure, but ambitions few embark upon and even fewer achieve.

We strive to do something and to be someone so that our life can have meaning before the sands of time fall in the hourglass. To do something and to be someone is an arduous task, but it can be done. Greatness can be achieved, though it may not be accomplished in insolation or without the benefit of an illustrious guide that will help illuminate through the often contentious and fractious world in which we live. For many, that illustrious guide is a philosophy of life, a phrase or statement that serves as a reminder of the type of values and ambitions they stand for, the type of person they hope to be, the type of world they hope to build.

The right philosophy of life can inspire a person and their generation to create a more noble and just world, and to become a more decent and honorable person. In an often more contentious and fractious world, three philosophies have served as the shining beacons in my life, inspiring me to be a better person and to make – in some small way – the world a better place. They are:

Always look for the good along the road of life.
Far too many search for what is wrong in life, focusing on the tribulations rather than the journeys and adventures, rather than what is right. One can lament on the isolated losses and failures, or marvel at the successes and victories that form the nucleus of a privileged life. To seek happiness rather than sadness, to offer admiration rather than criticism, to be appreciative rather than ungrateful, and to search for the good rather than the evil are all choices available to each and every one of us, if we so choose to make the right choice.

There are those who make the wrong choice and lead a tormented, vindictive, jealous and unhappy life. Their life is a consequence of evading rather than charging, playing rather than working, spending rather than saving, criticizing rather than praising, and blaming rather than accepting. Some forever look to their lack of money rather than their abundance of friends, their loss of a loved one rather than the good fortune to have people to love. Roses have thorns and parks have concrete; most focus on the pain of the thorns and ugliness of the concrete rather than the beauty of a rose or the beauty of the green grass.

Rarely do people pass through life unscathed: births are followed by deaths, some marriages end in divorce, bankruptcies may occur more frequently than windfalls. But nearly every person can see, hear, smell and walk. Most have sufficient food to eat, good health through their life, a job that affords a certain standard of living, friends to spend their time with, and are loved by someone and have someone to love. These may be the basics of life, but the appreciation of these basics serves as the cornerstone of a good life, the foundation upon which contentment and happiness are achieved.

Challenges are a surety in life, often having a debilitating effect on one's mind and body. Happiness or sadness, courage or fear, and being grateful or ungrateful all lie within our control. One cannot control every challenge in life, but all can control their response to these challenges. Follow the right path and live a life that is decent and honorable. Along the path, remember to forever be grateful for life's blessings and be grateful for the good along the road of life, for happiness and peace and not for what was achieved through any other means.

Go down swinging: the fear of failure, and the fear of what others think, has destroyed the ambitions of most men.
One of life's great tragedies is the many who reflect upon their life as a series of abandoned dreams and lost opportunities. Success and accomplishments are overshadowed by failures and disappointments. We seem to lament the cowardice we harbored rather than the courage we displayed, and that fact harkens of time wasted and promises unfulfilled, paralyzed minds and traumatized souls.

Regret is a circumstance common to those without the courage to stake their own claim in life, without the guts to follow their own ambitions, and without the resilience to persevere through any adversity or criticism in their path. Those that forsake all in the pursuit of noble and just ambitions are a solitary breed, unusually possessed of the fortitude foreign to most men. They display the unusual trait of fearlessness, of the ability to go down swinging for who they are, what they believe in, and where they intend to go.

The capacity and capability to go down swinging for one's life's ambitions is truly unique. For most, if not nearly all, life is limited by two fears: a fear of failure and a fear of what others think, both of which destroy one's ambitions. The pursuit of greatness and genuine goodness is often resisted by those at the other end of the moral spectrum, which is why those with uncommon decency stand in stark contrast to those with common bitterness. Jealousy, envy and selfishness are the foundational touchstones of those who applaud failures and ridicule actions of others, resulting in an unfulfilled person and an unremarkable life. Conversely, those who have learned that the fear of failure only arises through the pursuit of grand adventures, and that fear of what others think only arises from those without your best interests at heart, are those who eagerly go down swinging in the extraordinary pursuit that defines their existence.

Rise or fall, succeed or failure, win or lose, those that go down swinging change the course of their life. Moreover, those few who forsake the adversity, criticism and fear so prevalent in our society are the very few who change the course of history. It may be the singular most important pursuit of life: to pay any price and to bear any burden to chart your own course and light your own path. Take a chance and live your life: at the end of our time on Earth, the times that matter are those where you believed in something, worked for something, and went down swinging for something that was noble, that was just, and that was right. I hope you do not miss that opportunity.

Do something: if you spend your time doing good, maybe the Good Lord will let you stick around a bit longer.
Work and play, greedy and giving, love and hate. The world is replete with stark contrasts, of choices and consequences, of similarities and contradictions. One of life's grand mysteries is what someone should make of their life, of what they should do with their time on this Earth. We do not have the same opportunities as our neighbors, friends, or those in other countries, but everyone has an opportunity to improve upon the life into which they were born, to become a better person tomorrow than they were today, to make a difference – in some small way – with their time in this world. It is regrettable that so few take the opportunity to do so.

Some take the opportunity to pursue the most extensive educations, the riskiest of careers, the most intriguing of acquaintances, and the most fascinating of travels. These are interesting adventures, but they are not achievements. Education, careers, acquaintances and travels can be interesting adventures, but they are not achievements. They are not achievements because most never take the opportunity to **do something** with the education, careers, acquaintances, and travels once they are attained. They rest on those accomplishments, mistakenly believing that success is defined by what you have, not by what you do with what you have. Too many spend their life accumulating awards and honors in the hope that such decorations confer a sense of meaning; sadly, the pursuit of false idols is fleeting and rarely result in a feeling of meaning in one's life.

Achievements result from what you do with the life you were granted, of the life that you created. An accomplishment is obtaining a master's in public administration from USC; an achievement is using that knowledge to restructure and revitalize a local library so that children can learn to better read and write. An accomplishment is experiencing the wonders of the known world; an achievement is writing books and speeches on how different people can better live and work in peace and happiness. Accomplishments may make a person, but it is achievements that make a difference.

Those with the grandest achievements had the dream of a better world and the determination to make a difference. They also had the good fortune of time. No matter the idea, the hard work, or absence of fear, little is achieved without the time to do so – the one factor largely beyond our control. True, we can take calculated risks, eat well and exercise frequently, but we cannot control when the last tick of the clock will be struck. Until that time comes, then, we must always look for the good along the road of life, go down swinging for that which we believe in, and do something with what we have. More than anything, we should believe that the Man Upstairs believes in the noble work we strive to achieve, and the difference we are trying to make, and may let us stick around here on Earth just a little bit longer.

I have long believed that if you can dream the impossible dream, be determined to achieve it, never fear failure or what other people think, work hard, do what's right, and always look for the good in life, then you will have greatness within your grasp. Fame and fortune are not the determining factors of a great life, but rather that you fought the good fight, that you did the best you could with what you had, that you did what is right and that, in some small way, you make a difference. It has been a great ride, and for that I have been blessed.

In the dawn of life, we strive to make a living;

in the twilight of life, we strive to make a difference.

Section 2

THE KEY TO GREATNESS

It is becoming a more complicated world. Some struggle with personal battles and others struggle with professional struggles, but no matter the obstacles having a few core principles of philosophies can be of great guidance and comfort in an otherwise chaotic world. Here are my philosophies that may serve as a guide for your future happiness and success:

First is to **dream of a better future.** Dream of something great to achieve, no matter how unattainable – think of something different, make something better.

Second is to be **determined to achieve it.** Challenges, obstacles and barriers impede the ambitions of every life, and it is those very few that overcome their challenges, obstacles and barriers who can make a difference. For goodness sake, do something to achieve the dream.

Third is to **work hard** and remember that **results matter!** There are very, very few successful people who became successful without working hard. You may not have the right idea or the right job, but if you work hard you can nearly always succeed, and remember you are almost always judged by your results.

Fourth is to be **likeable.** Movie stars, sports heroes, and elected officials share one common trait: they are liked by their public. People enjoy watching, listening, and conversing with someone they like. It makes them feel good to spend time with someone they like, and the transgressions and wrongdoings committed by likeable people are often overlooked and condoned, simply because they are liked. Never underestimate the power of being likeable as you strive to change the world in which you live.

Fifth is the **guts to do the right thing.** Never evade, never betray, and never lie. Do the right thing at the right time and for the right reason, and you will improve the world, makes the world a better place, and live a decent and enviable life. Those very few go down swinging for what they believe in, knowing that the fear of failure, and the fear of what others think, has destroyed the ambitions of most people.

Finally is to **always look for the good.** Happiness or sadness, and being grateful or ungrateful, all lie within our control. One cannot control every challenge in life, but one can control their response to these challenges. Be ever grateful for the good that blesses your life, for happiness and peace and not for what was achieved through any other means.

Section 3

THE QUOTES

Always Look to the Good

**Quotes related to looking for the good
as we pass through life**

Next

Criticism rarely builds;
it almost always destroys

There are two types of people:
those who applaud efforts and those that applaud failures –
look for those who applaud your efforts.

You can control the way you live your life,
not the way others view your life

It is unfortunate, even sad, that some people's self-worth is determined
not through their own beliefs but through the jealous,
envious, and hateful opinions of others.

Being impervious to criticism may be uncommon to the many,
but it is common to the few, and it is those
few who truly change the world.

Never search for what is wrong;
search for what can be made right

You cannot do what is right unless you know what is right.

Honesty does not always pay
– you may win the election or triumph over adversity —

but dishonesty always costs
as relationships and friendships are destroyed,
and decency and honor lost,
all of which are rarely recovered.

Popularity and righteousness rarely coexist

Right always triumphs over wrong,
happiness always triumphs over sadness,
and good always triumphs over evil.

Educate the mind and you better the individual;
educate the soul and you better the world.

The road to happiness is an exhilarating quest,
one that is attainable to those with the drive and
desire to live a good and decent life.

Drama only belongs in a theater

Your worth is not determined by what you bring to the table;
your worth is determined by what you do once you are at the table

This country has progressed and its people prospered
because all shared the principles of its shared culture:
that you obey the laws and pay your taxes,
that you are a kind and honorable person,
that you work hard and can keep most of what you earn,
that you share what you have with the less fortunate,
and that you strive to make the world a better place.

Though the allure of a better life may be tarnished
this remains a country where dreams can come true –
a country that rescued the world for democracy in World War II,
invented the computer and the Internet,
and created the polio and flu vaccines that
have helped countless millions.

And, it still remains a country capable of resurrecting
the fabled ideals of its historic past by creating a new society
in which its people are only limited by their imaginations
and their willingness to bear any burden in
their pursuit of the American Dream.

Section 4

THE QUOTES

Go Down Swinging

**Quotes related to going down swinging
as you pursue a life of purpose**

Talent will get you in the top 100
Hard work will get you in the top 10
Guts will get you to the top

They have to live that life

No matter what someone says or does towards you,
it says more about them than about you.
Hate begets hate, and kindness begets kindness,
and those that choose of the path of hate and negativity
are destined to follow that unfortunate path.

"They have to live that life," not you.
Never let the rude, mean, hateful, and negative comments
about you from others affect your life,
for they are the only ones who have to live that type of life.

Just trying to make a living

Be true to your own ambitions, pursue something important to you,
and you will never experience failure…

for there is never any shame in trying, in giving your best,
in extending every effort in the pursuit of
something that defines who you are.

If you don't like the ride, try another amusement park

The fear of failure, the fear of success, the fear of uncertainty,
the fear of losing friends and family, the fear of honesty, and the
most destructive fear of all, the fear of what others think….

These fears create doubt and uncertainty and paralyze one's ambition.
For what? So you do not lose? So people like you?

I would rather lose everything as I pursue
my own dreams and aspirations
than win nothing because I settled and pursued
someone else's dream or aspiration.

Never say time ran out; be able to say you used
every second of time you were granted.

Never say you lacked talent or the ability to win;
be able to say you used all you were granted
and left everything on the field.
And, never say you were afraid of failure; be
able to say you had the courage to try.

This is the mark of someone who can look back, as the years progress,
on a life that had purpose, on a life that has been
lived, and on a life that made a difference.

Great accomplishments,
and great rewards,
often come from great sacrifice.

Never waiver, never falter;
never give in, never give up;
on that which is your destiny

Follow your passion in life,
no matter the adversity of criticism encountered

Our country has become a society not of independent
frontiersmen but dependent citizens,
not of those seeking a hand up but those seeking a handout,
not of those accepting responsibility for their own actions
but looking to blame others for their poor choices,
not of those working for the nation's interest
but seeking their own self-interest,
and not of appreciation for life's blessings but of
jealousy and envy for those who have more.

The "rugged individual" that once defined Americans has abdicated
their responsibility to control their own destiny.

They are now utterly dependent on an employer for a job,
the government for health care and retirement,
and the wealthy to pay this nation's taxes,
creating a deepening sense of insecurity and instability
throughout its economic, political and societal institutions.

Whereas success once meant you had the opportunity
to "pull up" on the ladder of success,
today more want to "pull down" those above them on that ladder.

There is, for the most part, an equality of opportunity;
there is not, however, an equality of ambition

Too many believe money should be redistributed
because it was earned unfairly;
too few believe it has been distributed rightfully
because it was earned fairly.

The simple truth is that – with very few exceptions –
money is not earned by greedy, selfish, deceitful, and
dishonest people, or through birth or luck.
Instead, money is earned by those who
have sacrificed the greatest, risked the most, studied
the longest, and worked the hardest.

Who is more selfish:

the person who wants to keep the money they earned,
or the person who wants to take the money someone else earned.

Those who believe money is the root of all evil
and has led to the destruction of society
are the same people who demand that same money be redistributed
from those that have earned it, to those who have not.

It seems the successful are good enough to earn the money,
just not good enough to spend it.

Rare is the individual who is accountable for his or her actions
and takes responsibility for the unfortunate choices made throughout life

The truth is that we have far more power to control
our future than others do to destroy it.

We have the ability to study more, save more, invest
more, exercise more, and work more.
We have the strength to waste less, drink less, smoke less, and sin less,
and the capacity to restrain our ego, jealousy, and envy.

We are not victims of circumstances: with few
exceptions, those who became successful did so
because they capitalized on their opportunities, not
because they took advantage of others.

Yet too many seem to have abdicated their responsibility
to determine their own destiny in life,
and instead seek to blame others for the lot in
life that is often of their own choosing.

Blame, though, has never solved a problem—
it simply shields a person from accepting responsibility for it,
and is the avenue of choice for cowards unwilling to take a chance,
lacking in fortitude to take a stand, and unwilling to make a difference

Justice is a certainty.

Life is not fair; a fair only exists for clowns and elephants.

In the end, we live in one of history's great countries,
which offers everyone the freedom of achievement or misfortune,
of work or leisure, of determination or laziness,
of success or failure, and of wealth or poverty.

The opportunities are plentiful, if one chooses to take them.

Section 5

THE QUOTES

Do Something

Quotes related to doing something with your time on Earth

The seminal economic event of the last century —

the event that has destabilized the middle class
and led to a widening disparity between the fortunate and unfortunate—

is this country's inability to produce and manufacture goods and services
that afford its citizens a good job at a good wage.

The grand experiment of liberal government –

that a larger and more powerful government
providing an ever-expanding growth
in benefits and services would produce a safe, fair,
just, harmonious, and utopian society –

has been an abject failure, a determining factor
in the decline of a once great country.

Taxes are an expense of a business entity and its owner alike.
Additional taxes paid by a business and its owner
translates into an expense that must be paid,
a reason virtually all taxes are passed onto the consumer.

And in an ironic twist of fate, taxes encourages
the outsourcing of American jobs –
the very taxes intended to bring "fairness"
in terms of income distribution
raises the price of American goods against lower-taxed countries –
forcing companies to seek lower-cost countries
to produce their goods and services.

The once noble and decent profession of politics has
degenerated into decadence and incivility,
where deflecting blame is more important than reflecting character.

Rather than elected officials reflecting the best in America and
working to create a more decent and honorable
country for future generations,
they represent the worst in America—
societal divisiveness, selfishness, careless disregard for future generations,
and a lack of personal accountability and responsibility.

In so many ways, we are getting exactly the
type of government we deserve,
just not one that we need.

Political problems are solved by innovative and well-reasoned ideas,
along with the willingness to pay any price and bear any burden
to implement those ideas to an often unwilling and ungrateful public

We are limited only by the dream of a better world
and the determination to make a difference.

Spend your time reaching for the stars, even
if you just miss touching them...
for it is the majesty of your dreams, and the force of your determination,
that gives purpose to your journey and meaning to your life.

Too many have spent more than they have saved,
used more than they have had,
and taken more than they have given.

They have made a life, but not a difference,
and that disappointment and regret haunts their soul.

Everyone has something they wish they did not have;
the real challenge is to do something with what you do have.

Ultimately, you must DO something in order to BE something

Organizations and employees that assess the
future and can adapt to its eventuality
remain at the forefront of success

Every person is given a platform: a teacher, a singer, a carpenter.

What you do with that platform determines
the pride in your past,
the happiness in your present,
and the legacy for your future.

Your life is not judged by what you take when you are here,
but by what you leave when you are gone.

It matters little whether your aspiration or dream was realized:
we will never have global peace, or feed the world's hungry,
or avoid catastrophic diseases or illnesses.

What matters is that you tried, for the crowning glory of man
is to leave the world a little bit better than how he found it

To make a difference, you must change the world;
to change the world, you must change yourself.

Live your life so that you have made the most
out of everything you were given,
that you persevered over those illnesses and financial
setbacks to make the most of your life,
that you dedicated your life to make the most of
your physical talents and mental abilities.

That, when the game we call life nears its end,
we can proudly and honestly say that
"we did the best we could with everything we were given"
and we reached our potential as human beings
and contributed everything possible to the betterment of mankind.

We endeavor to live life so that our family and
friends can say at our funeral that

"some may have thought he had a tough life,
and yes, he did have obstacles.
But he did the best he could with what he had,
he did the right thing at the right time and for the right reason,
and he fought the good fight.

Now here rests a good person who led a decent and honorable life,
a person now surrounded by a life well lived
and by the people he touched along his journey.
We have been blessed to know this man,
and we have been fortunate that this man
has made our world just a little bit better by his life."

Section 6

THE LISTS

THE GOOD ORGANIZATION

Nearly everyone works for someone else, and the more successful you become the larger the organization becomes. Since organizations need "fewer and fewer of better and better workers," so says Michael Hammer, creating and sustaining an effective organization is central to success. In that light, here are the components of successful organizations:

First is **imagination** – in other words, they have created an organization that facilitates the generation and promotion of ideas throughout the organization. The imagination of today becomes the reality of tomorrow.

Second is that this imagination leads to a **competitive advantage**, that one thing (quality, price, techniques, etc.) that they do better than anyone else, and the public is willing to pay for that competitive advantage.

Third are **superstars**, meaning the organization has talent dedicated to the promotion of the company. Talent does not mean that "you are born with it or not born with it," but rather you hire and retain the best in their field and put them in the right position.

Fourth is that **customers are the focus of everything** that they do, so that any action or decision is predicated on how it affects the customer, or how it generates new customers.

Fifth is an **obsession with quality** so that their product, or service, must always be better today than it was yesterday. And, most importantly, they must be working to make it even better tomorrow.

Sixth is that they **do what's right**. Effective organizations know that customers, and employees, want to be associated with people who will treat them fairly and that can be trusted. When you buy a product or service, you are also buying the organization's reputation, a reputation where the organization constantly does the right thing and goes far to develop trust with those it does business with.

These actions may not guarantee an effective organization, but few organizations attain success without sustaining what is referred to above.

THE GOOD MANAGER

In nearly any profession or position that you hold, you have some type of management responsibility whether it is fulfilling a customer's order or overseeing employees. Given how challenging the profession often seems, a good manager ultimately boils down to a few simple, common attributes, which are:

First is that good managers **like what you do**. Management is an exhilarating experience that allows you to have a greater role in the development and success of an employee and an organization.

Second is to **know your job**. Managers with the greatest breadth and depth of knowledge simply have a better opportunity to make a more reasoned and intelligent decision on a wide range of organizational issues, from the hiring of an employee to the development of the organization's strategic plan.

Third are **solid organizational skills**. There are certain basic building blocks of a manager's competence (including planning, delegating, and managing time) that must be mastered.

Fourth is to **work hard**. There are very, very few successful people who became successful without working hard. You may not have the right idea or the right job, but if you work hard you can almost always succeed.

Fifth is to **make work fun**. Most people yearn for fun in their life, for a time and place where they feel comfortable and are welcomed regardless of their challenges and difficulties.

Sixth is to **be a good person**. The most important attribute of a good manager is to be a good person: incredibly kind-hearted, controls their most destructive human emotions, tells the truth, does what's right, and always looks for the good along the road of life. As employees search for the perfect job in the perfect career, look first for a manager that is a kind and generous person. As organizations search for the most talented managers, look first for a decent and honorable person who has only the purest and noblest intentions for the employees. Inevitably, I believe our happiness or unhappiness in the workplace depends on finding that good person. Never settle until you find that person.

THE GOOD TEACHER

Education is one of the most important investments in nearly any society; in California alone, the state commits about 40 percent of its budget to educational pursuits. Nearly every study indicates that teachers are the most valuable instrument in the educational choir, so it may be helpful to converse about the traits and attributes that make a "good" teacher and/or a "great" teacher. These include:

First is to **have a passion to teach**. It is not just a job, but their life's ambition. This passion to use education for the betterment of others fuels their relentless drive to disregard the status quo and constantly challenge those in education to create a more diverse, creative, and effective institution.

Second is that **they care** about their profession, their school, their students, and their community. They care that students are physically well, have a decent meal, complete their homework, and are safe within the confines of the school. They care that parents are involved and that the community participates in the educational enterprise. They care that staff are adequately compensated and have the tools to accomplish their job.

Third is an extraordinary level of **energy and enthusiasm**. Those districts often cited as the model for others have a high degree of participation from its constituents and a level of energy and enthusiasm that translates into a "can do, will do" attitude that permeates all its interactions.

Fourth is that they **make education fun**. Similar to dinner with friends, you tend to participate more when there is an element of fun associated with the venture. Sports are an appropriate analogy here. Most will participate in some level of sporting event because there is an element of fun. It is the journey they enjoy as much as the attainment of their goal. In education, whether it be diversity or academic achievements, effective leaders are those that structure their environment to include a high degree of fun associated with social interactions and learning.

EFFECTIVE HUMAN RESOURCES

There are many "effective" lists that you can review when you want to learn to be better at something, or when you seek to obtain a job but are unsure about the principle aspects you should concentrate on. In that light, I wanted to list the most important skills and abilities of a human resource professional. In any case, it will get the conversation started:

First is an **expert in HR fundamentals**, including recruitment, compensation, classification, benefits processing, discipline, and workers compensation, etc. It is impossible to be success in human resources if you are unaware and uninformed on the most effective trends and techniques associated with human resources.

Second is the ability to **translate HR fundamentals to business success** in your chosen organization. Successful human resource professionals/ departments are able to use recruitments, compensation, strategic planning and other tools within their "human resources toolkit" to add value and worth to the organization, thereby raising the profile and respect of the human resources profession.

Third is to **build relationships** by being **likeable, nice and fun** – this builds relationships, which is a core function of human resources. A majority of the HR profession is concerned with building relationships, you must be someone that people want to work with, and can be trusted, so that you can build relationships during negotiations, hiring, health concerns, organizational policies and their effect, and discipline.

Fourth is to have **absolute credibility**. Tell the truth and never, ever compromise what you believe in because once lost your credibility can never be regained.

Fifth is to **always be right**. Human resources deals with the most sensitive aspect of a person's life, from their hiring to their health to their salary. If you make the wrong promotion or discipline the wrong person you can affect a person and their family for the rest of their life, and it does destroy your own credibility. Therefore, you must always be right by consulting often and widely, benchmarking your approach, and then making a reasoned decision based on a studious and unbiased inquiry.

EFFECTIVE PUBLIC RELATIONS

Public relations is concerned with how you influence your environment, whether that be your employees or customers. Creating, and sustaining, the right image is crucial to customer and employees attraction/retention. The most effective public relations techniques to create that right image would include:

First is to **remember you only get one shot**. Whatever action or statement you make, you can rarely change it and maintain your credibility.

Second is to **anticipate the inevitable**. A situation may arise that may be challenging, but often times we do not know the full depth of the issue. The "other" shoe will inevitably drop. Know the full issue before you respond.

Third is to have a **clear command of oral/ written skills**. Speak and write confidently to garner the credibility your position demands.

Fourth is to **use various media** to promote your agenda, from Facebook to the web to Twitter. Be able to use the most appropriate medium in the appropriate situation.

Fifth, and possibly the most important, **always tell the truth**. If you do not know the answer, say so. If you cannot give the answer, artfully tell your audience you cannot divulge that information. Once you lose the trust of your audience (whether that be the press or the general public), your career is largely finished.

Sixth is to **always maintain a controlled and positive demeanor.** As the old saying goes, "never let them see you sweat." Be able to maintain your composure no matter what the issue is or the direction it is going in.

EFFECTIVE TEAMS

In our world, the function and use of teams offers a country a particular competitive advantage. The greatest example is Japan, which focuses on the use of teamwork in order to accomplish an objective. Corporations, too, recognize the importance of teams. In general, the greatest benefit of teams is the elicitation, and contribution, of individuals with different thoughts and opinions. These differences allow a team to think and be different, and it is that difference where new ideas and products/services are developed. The team, then, can work towards harnessing those contributions in the development of that new product/service.

Teams come with problems, of course. They can take longer to arrive at a decision, feud among members, relationships can suffer if conflicts and disagreements are mishandled, there may be a rush to accomplishment, and everyone starts to think the same. But those problems are diminished when you can build an effective team, the components of which would include:

First is to **hire the right people**. Remember that good football coaches do not choose players at random and hope they will be effective athletes. Bring talent to the team and it will flourish.

Second is to have a **common purpose that is deemed worthwhile to accomplish**. Individuals, and teams, work harder when they want what they work for.

Third is to **utilize the strengths and minimize the weaknesses of each team member**. Take advantage of what each member's talent and ability is while limiting the damage that can be done by each member's lack of talent and ability.

Fourth is to **have clear rules of behavior and performance.** Work must be completed as required, meetings attended as requested, and conduct exhibited as expected.

Fifth is to **make the task of the team, and the time spent within the team, as fun as possible**. Work implies drudgery and effort; create a fun environment where people genuinely like spending time with each other and your task will almost always be met, if not exceeded.

Clear goals, talented people, and a fun time. The world can be changed with that type of team.

EFFECTIVE CUSTOMER SERVICES

There are few people who do not have a customer in one shape or form. Most achieve success because they have a customer to serve, whether that is the president of the United States (who serves this country's citizens) or the famous movie star (who serves their fans). So knowing how best to serve the customer is one of the best avenues to a more secure future. Specific actions that may result in a strong relationship with a customer include:

First is to **you have a job because you have a customer**. Without a customer, you are without a job. The customer is not always right, but the customer is the customer.

Second is to **give the customer more than they expect**. Be a cab driver who opens the door for their customer, a hair salon that sends a card on your birthday, or a dry cleaner that replaces a button without a charge.

Third is to **give customers a reason to come back**: offer a coupon, discount, points for each purchase. This establishes a relationship with the customer, in addition to loyalty and force of habit.

Fourth is to **bounce back quickly**. A simple mistake or oversight can hurt a customer's perception (e.g., car is not ready, or the steak is well-done, not rare) but only if it is not overcome quickly by fixing the problem and giving the customer a care token (for instance, a garage gives you a loaner or the restaurant buys your dessert).

Fifth is to **do not worry about the sale, worry about the relationship**. Talking a customer out of a purchase because it is not right for them develops trust between the seller and the buyer. The buyer believes you actually care about them, rather than simply care about the sale. They will then be more trusting of your advice and counsel in the future, and tell others that you are an ethical and moral company to do business with. This means you do the right thing, at the right time, and for the right reason.

FOUR TYPES OF EMPLOYEES

Hiring and retaining the most talented and productive employees is central to organizational productivity and profitability. Finding the most talented and productive can be an adventure, and in this search for the best and the brightest it seems that employees fall into one of four categories:

First are the **superstars.** These are the most important, and valuable, members of the organization. They generate the ideas and actions that propel the organization forward. They should be paid more, treated differently, and retained at all costs.

Second are the **doers.** These are people that perform their job well. They do not generate outstanding ideas or are naturally creative, but often "put into action" the thoughts and ideas of the superstars. They do the work and that work is important for the organization.

Third are the **plodders.** These are the average employees who do just enough to complete their job. More effort should be directed toward hiring doers rather than plodders, but there exists a level of plodders in any organization.

Fourth are the **slugs.** These individuals should be "encouraged" to leave the organization. They are a drain on resources and affect productivity and profitability, and almost certainly morale as well. Today's organization cannot accept slugs anywhere in the organization.

It is the superstars that deserve the awards and accolades, and doers are a requirement to get the job done. Plodders and slugs continue to affect an organization to a negative degree and those employees should be "encouraged" to find work in other organizations. That may seem harsh or insensitive, but the realities of today's marketplace requires nearly all employees to contribute within the organization or the organization as a hole cannot be sustained.

RULES OF EMPLOYEE CONDUCT

Organizations have ethics, homes have morals, and businesses have rules. It is business that provide the manner in which employees conduct themselves, and it is an employee's dedication to follow these rules through the course of their employment that can ultimately determine an organization's productivity and profitability. These rules include:

First is that **truth is an absolute defense** – eventually, a "cover-up" becomes "uncovered" and the repercussions are more significant than if you would have acknowledged the issue and took your "lumps." Additionally, the further you deviate from the truth, the more exposure you encounter. Be honest and straightforward; your reputation will survive better than if you damage your character and credibility.

Second, **it is not what you know but what you can prove**. It does not matter what you hear, see or feel; in the end it is only what you can prove. This may force you to temper your requests/demands, but it is better to win small than lose big.

Third is that **it depends**. Rarely are issues completely right or wrong; there is a bit of doubt in almost every issue. Listen, research, review options, and all the while clearly state your options are predicated on certain facts known and others unknown.

Fourth is that **if it's not a hill, don't climb it**. Be interested in those things that matter to you. Control your ego and self-interest and when you do make a stand it will be for an important event or circumstance.

Fifth is to remember that **life is not fair**. Others may be more rich, handsome, beautiful, or successful, and there is really no reason why. Let the "but it is not fair" argument go, and you will open up your life. "Fair" is a place where they have elephants and serve peanuts; it is not common that you will encounter circumstances, events, or people who treat you as fair as they do others. The trick in life is to overcome those burdens and mistreatments that truly are a fact of life. Be concerned with yourself, and you will find that life really is fairer than you ever realized. With that, I wish you the best in life!

THE KEYS TO REASONED JUDGMENT

Reasoned and sound judgment is more of an art than a science in that there is not one prescribed approach to make the perfect decision. There are, however, several aspects that should be considered before deciding on an action to take. These aspects, called the "Keys to Reasoned Judgment," are as follows:

First is to clearly **define the issue** at hand. Solve the right problem, not the wrong situation.

Second is to **state the key "knowns"** or "facts" of the case. This forces you to think through the issue and determine the important "knowns" of the case and to gather relevant facts, statistics, and theories. Remember that by stating the "knowns" in writing you are better able to follow the outline of the problem.

Third is to **state the key "unknowns"** of the case. Only when you "know what you do not know" can you ensure you have thought through the problem. You may not know the answer, but if you know the question you can tell your audience you thought about that key question but the answer (or data, or information) could not be found or resolved. Additionally, if any of these unknown facts are later known, you will be able to revise your judgment.

Fourth is to **state the credible assumptions** based on the known and unknown facts. Assumptions are foundational components on most decisions (for instance, you may not "see" an individual walk into the building, but if they are in the building you can assume they entered through some door or window; if someone is walking out of a department store with their shopping bag you may assume they purchased something from that store). Assumptions are components and considerations in decision making because one rarely has perfect information.

Fifth is to make a **deliberate and sound decision** based on the previous four considerations.

By controlling one's emotions and impulses – and concentrating on the Keys to a Reasoned Judgment approach – a more balanced and reasoned judgment can be realized, leading to greater influence in one's personal and professional lives.

THE ART OF MOTIVATING EMPLOYEES

Motivation is an individual's inner state that causes them to behave in a way that ensures the accomplishment of some goal. It is a set of psychological processes that energizes voluntary behavior; it is the reason for which people exert and expend effort on activities that reward them. Contrary to common wisdom, managers cannot motivate an employee: they can only create a workplace environment that will inspire employees to perform. For instance: an all-expense paid trip to the Bahamas for the top salesperson will only motivate those who want to go to the Bahamas. Therefore, find out what employees want, provide it to them, and that is the genius of motivation.

Motivation, then, is not an illusion. Employees can be motivated to perform by management that are cognizant of the following strategies:

First is to **know the wants and desires of employees.** As mentioned, find out what someone wants and then try to give it to them.

Second is to create a **job that is interesting and challenging.** People want to be in control of their future; allow them that and they are better motivated to perform.

Third is to **provide a fair wage and recognition.** Few aspects demotivate an employee more than being underpaid and underappreciated.

Fourth is to **believe that their work serves others.** The more employees believe in what they do, and how it can make a difference, the more excited they will be to perform.

Fifth is to **create a fun place to work.** Like chocolate and amusement parks, people who like something are constantly excited about doing it. Create a fun place for employees to work and their performance will reflect this excitement.

Hire the right person and create the right environment – these are actions firmly within management's purview and form the basis of motivated employees and a productive workforce.

THE ART OF MAKING THE RIGHT DECISION

We see education and experience as a reservoir of knowledge to make the right decision. It is not an easy task, but life is a series of significant and insignificant circumstances. Those that make the right choices in the most significant circumstances have a better chance of obtaining their ambitions. The ability to make the right choices, the right decisions, focusses on the following process:

First is that you must have the desire and **will to be right**. The effort must be expended to ensure that you will acquire the research wherever it may take you.

Second is that you must deliberately and diligently **follow a systematic approach**/guideline through the process; this can be accomplished by developing a rubric that reminds/forces you to address each aspect, thus ensuring you do not forget any important steps, but yet relays to your audience that the process followed was well-thought out, thus indicating competence.

Third is that any **findings have to be related to the evidence** (another important Socratic requirement). You should not state, "I believe" or "it is my opinion that," but rather "one can reasonably conclude, based on the evidence obtained, that..." This adds incredible influence to your arguments when your findings are predicated on facts, statistics, theories, etc.

Fourth is to **control your biases and emotions**, because when you allow other factors than the evidence, to control either the process or the findings, you undermine your reputation as a reasoned thinker and thereby it affects your influence.

Fifth is to **always look at the other side**. If your finding was that something should be done, ask yourself why it has not been done before or, more importantly, why would others say it should not be done. Anticipate the arguments against your findings before they are published and be prepared to dispute their main points.

Sixth is to be **respectful of others** whose point of view/beliefs are different than your own. Their position may not be reasonable or logical, but acrimonious times often result more from the way you treat people rather than your findings. Allow people to save face, be fair and reasonable, and you will more often than not find that spirited debates are not harmful to a long-term, mutually beneficial business relationship.

THE ART OF FINDING A JOB

These are certainly challenging times for most anyone looking for a job. There are many poor paying jobs available yet few good paying jobs. Finding the good job requires considerable dedication/hard work along with possessing the right talents/qualifications for the right position. These strategies offer the best strategies in order to find, apply and obtain the good job in these challenging times.

First is that it is **always easier to get a job when you have one**. You tend to be more confident and assured when you have a job during the interview process; without a job, a candidate seems to try too hard, mainly because they have so much riding on getting that job.

Second is that it **takes one month to get a job for every $10,000 you want to make** a year. If you are looking for a job that pays $100,000, it will generally take you about 10 months to find that job. The main reason for the length of time is that there are fewer jobs that pay $100,000 a year, and of course more people trying to find that job. So, if you are planning to find a job, recognize that it is going to take you a considerable period of time to find it.

Third is to **offer something unique** to your future employer. Whenever the job market becomes more challenging, it is those people who have the most to offer that tend to get those jobs. So, invest in yourself, create your own research and development account so that you can continually pay to acquire the additional skills and knowledge that will make you the most qualified person for any position that you feel is within your grasp.

Fourth is that **it takes drive and ambition**, guts and determination to keep applying, to keep trying, to never let yourself get down, to always believe that the next job is yours and it will be everything that you have hoped for. If you can have that attitude and tenacity, you may not get the next job, or the one after that, but you will surely get the job you want and need at some point in the near future.

Your career dreams can come true, but you do need to do something about fulfilling them. You cannot just hope for the future, you must work for the future that you want.

MANAGING YOUR TIME

Why do we manage time? We manage time because we want to do something with our life. Unless you have time you have no reason to organize yourself because you have nowhere to go and nothing to accomplish. It then makes no difference how long anything takes.

In reality, managing your time is a fairly simplistic concept. The following strategies are intended to provide focus to your day and ensure each second is devoted to something of importance. These strategies include:

First is to **get rid of useless tasks and activities**. Ask "why does this need to be done" and "what do we get when it is done." If you do not know the answer, or its value is minimal, get rid of the task.

Second is to **use small amounts of tasks.** Maybe the most important time management strategy – it is the five minutes before work, on the bus, waiting for dinner, sitting in the car, lying in bed…five minutes soon adds to 50 minutes or more per day, a great amount of time.

Third is to **improve your reading and writing skills.** Too many people waste time because they have not yet perfected their reading and writing abilities.

Fourth is to **keep one list**. Allows one to prioritize their tasks and to never forget what is important. Send yourself emails and phone alarms as reminders of what needs to be done, and by what time.

Fifth is to **use the telephone rather than emails.** Not only does the telephone build relationships, but little is lost in the translation; whereas emails often require many attempts before the true message/intent is received.

Finally is to **start the day with the most important task**. This action reduces stress and negativity because the most important task is completed first and cannot be derailed by unexpected delays or crisis during the day.

Time is the mechanism that allows you to achieve your ambitions, and the better use of time the better chance you have of achieving something great.

THE ART OF THE RESUME

A resume is a written history of who you are. It does not state who you will be, but rather collective statements on what you have done which, if presented correctly, can lead a prospective employer to imagine what you will become. The resume, then, becomes a vehicle that determines your path in life, and it assumes even greater importance in today's increasingly competitive job environment. The best resumes are cognizant of the following:

First is that a resume must be bold and **exciting to read**. It should be clean and easy to read – the number of words/bullets kept to a minimum and quite a bit of "white space," or unused space, so that it appears professional and neat.

Second is to make sure the resume **mirrors the job announcement/** advertisement. Be truthful, and hopefully what they are looking for in the job announcement is evidenced in your resume. Use key phrases/words from the announcement in your resume, which means your resume must be modified for each position you apply.

Third is to **highlight accomplishments** rather than duties. It is not what you were supposed to do, but what you did, that captures the interest of an employer. Examples include: reduced expenditures 10% by streamlining..... increased sales 10% by reorganizing operations to include...

Fourth is that resume information is placed **in order of importance**. If your education raises your value, list education first. Same with bullets: include the most important accomplishment first, then others in descending importance (keep bullets to 3-5 per instance otherwise you dilute their importance).

Fifth is to **highlight your stability and balance**. Be careful of working less than 2-3 years per job; only include "year" of employment rather than "months" so calculating your limited experience is more challenging. Additionally, include information that showcases a well-rounded background such as contributing to society (e.g., Special Olympics) and group memberships (e.g., Rotary Club), books. The highlights should show a "balanced" individual who is interested in more than money or status. In an era of social responsibility within organizations, this is an important attribute.

Sixth is to **include a cover letter** which is another avenue for you to convey information to the resume reviewer that highlights how your skills/ knowledge/abilities are related to their job announcement.

In a resume, care must be exercised to be honest, straight-forward, and keep a keen eye toward what the reviewer is expecting to see. Create a resume where the reviewer says, "I need to meet this person" and you gain the important "foot in the door."

THE ART OF INTERVIEWING

There are some that spend considerable time and effort to locate the ideal job, submit an impressive resume and cover letter, and then meet disaster in the interview. Interviewing can be a daunting and intimidating experience, mainly because others are judging your worth and some are insecure with their accumulated history. There are several strategies you utilize to present yourself well in an interview.

First is to **prepare, prepare, and prepare**. Read the job description and the job announcement, study what the organization is looking for, review your past accomplishments and current abilities, and commit everything to memory. Spend three times as much time in studying for an interview than you would for a college test, and study three times more! You will never be nervous about what you know, which should alleviate some nervousness in the interview.

Second is simple: **get them to like you**. People want to work with people they like, so be as personable as you can be. Smile, be friendly, stay positive and energetic – never underestimate the power of likeability in being selected for a job.

Third is to **dress respectfully and appropriately** for the job. Neat is often an inexpensive way to present yourself well.

Fourth is to **convey why you are is THE best person for the job**. Interviewers want to know why they should hire you, so tell them exactly why they should.

Fifth is to **feel like you have something important to say**. If you feel like you have something important to say or to contribute to the organization, that passion will be infectious and you will present yourself as THE person for the job.

Sixth is to **never care what others say**. The reason most are nervous in an interview is because they feel like they are being judged (similar to public speaking). If you are a good person and a qualified candidate, never worry about how you present yourself.

Seventh is to **always be honest**. If you are honest and the organization does not choose you, at least you know that job is not for you. If you are not honest and they choose you, they may have been looking for someone else and, if you are hired based on who you are not, it could end badly.

In all, remember there are millions of jobs in the world. If you are not selected for that job – and you have worked to become a talented, hardworking, and likeable person – rest assured the perfect job is only an interview or two away.

THE ART OF PUBLIC SPEAKING

One of the most daunting, daring, and exhilarating aspects of leadership is public speaking. More fear speaking than nearly any other duty or task; in reality, there are a few simple strategies that one can follow to greatly enhance their ability to deliver an informative and inspiring presentation. These include:

First is that you must **believe you have something important to say**. When you feel you have something important to say, you develop the confidence to deliver your words with passion.

Second is that you **do not care what other people think**. One of the principle reasons so many fear public speaking is because they are afraid of what people are going to say. If you do the right thing, for the right reason and at the right time, then you should not care what anyone else will say.

Third is to totally and absolutely **know your materials.** Nerves may enter into public speaking, but do not be nervous about whether you know your subject/speech.

Fourth is to **make it fun**. Be energetic, smile, and include the audience. They will be drawn into your presence, especially since a typical presentation is judged 55% by how you look, 38% by how you talk, and only 7% by what you say.

Fifth is to remember that **first and last impressions are everything**. The two most important parts of your presentation are the first 30 and the last 15 seconds. You may want to use ice-breakers (short, appropriate, participate) concentrate on capturing your audience in the first few seconds, and then leaving them with something memorable at its end.

Always remember public speaking is your time to say something valuable to someone, so I hope you take that opportunity.

THE ART OF NEGOTIATIONS

Whether managing relations between management and labor, bargaining and bartering, building contracts and settling disputes, conversing with advisors and friends, or making deals, the ability to negotiate in a fair, reasonable, and honest manner largely determines your reputation as a person and, ultimately, your success as a professional. Negotiating is an "art," meaning there is not one true way to success and you must adjust your methods to a given situation; however, there are a few strategies that will serve nearly everyone well as they negotiate their path through life. These include:

First is to be **honest and keep your word**. Build a reputation for being fair but firm, and those that interact with you will respect you, your position, and have trust in what you say and what you can deliver.

Second is to **keep emotions in check**. One rarely wins every argument, and one is certain to lose a battle or two during the course of time. But once the deal is done – no matter the manner in which the other side conducted themselves – uncontrolled emotions betray your character. Instead, devote your energies to the next battle, be fully aware of mistakes made and the true character of the opposing side.

Third is to **know what the other side wants**. If you know what they truly want – not just what they say – both sides can actively search for a resolution to the problem at hand.

Fourth is to **know every facet and fact of the negotiations**. Know the law, policy, history, culture, and politics – the more you know, the more options you can create.

Fifth is to **know when to take a stand**. Have patience, avoid fighting a losing battle, and take a stand on only the most critical, fundamental issues – the rest can be negotiated.

Sixth is to **ensure the other side believes they won**. If one believes they "won" they are more likely to "make the deal." Control your own ego and let others appear to be the victor, for if you accomplish the objectives of the negotiations you are as much a winner as anyone.

Results matter

Section 7

THE STORIES

WHAT DEFINES YOU

What defines you…for a few it is a statement, some an action, and others an accomplishment. As the years remaining are fewer than the years past, we contemplate that statement, action or accomplishment that will define our time on Earth.

Defining yourself means the characteristic or traits that you possess that give a picture, or a map, of who you are. It is best, then, to first determine who you want to be, and then strive to become that person. For instance, if you want to be a person who is honest and straightforward, then you do need to make the tough, often conflict-generating comments to people that indicate first, you have their interests at heart and, second, you offer your thoughts and criticisms so that they can improve themselves.

Similarly, if you want to be a person who gives back more than they take, you will have to devote some of your time to some type of charity or devotion to others. This means that you will have to sacrifice your own time, and your personal wealth (in some cases), but the rewards that could arise from these actions would be even more rewarding.

In all, you must first choose the type of person you want to be known for, and the type of person that you feel would represent yourself well to others. Then, live the type of life that allows that to come true. What defines you is really quite easy: it is knowing that you have control over what you will become, though it will often take hard work and sacrifice to ultimately be that type of person. A person of honor, a person of giving, a person of accomplishment – all those are noble endeavors that will define your existence and give meaning to your time on Earth.

CONTRIBUTE

Though we each have challenges in life, most would agree that they lead an enviable, charmed life. Whether it be their health, intelligence, family, friends, a job, or any other shining star in their life, we are more fortunate than we ever realize. Unfortunately for some, they do not realize or appreciate their good fortune; they also do not realize the expectation that they have as a member of society.

What is that expectation? It is to contribute, in some small way, to bettering the world. There are many who may say they do not have the time, the energy, the money, or the ability to do so. For a very few, that may be true. For many, though, it simply is not true. It is difficult to claim you cannot deliver meals once a month to those who cannot leave their home; to time races for those participating in Special Olympics; or to play the piano during the Holiday Season at a retirement home.

In these instances, you contribute your unique talents and help others. While it may be claimed that others benefit from your generosity, in reality it is you that benefit the most. Your self-esteem and pride in your contributions make you a better person, one who will go through life recognizing that you do not always take from what life has to offer, but leave something behind as well.

So, as you go through life, remember the importance of contributing to those whose life may not shine as bright as yours. In doing so, you certainly make the world a better place to live, but more importantly, you make yourself a better person to know.

LOYALTY

Does loyalty exist in today's workplace? Sadly for some, loyalty has become a bygone relic of days gone by for a number of reasons. First is that the nature of society has changed. With international competition and the need for increased efficiency, one could be an outstanding employee yet be unemployed because your firm can no longer compete in its market/industry. Therefore, the relentless pursuit of lower-cost manufacturing and service ensures very few individuals will obtain job security. Without job security, there is little to keep an employee there over the long term.

Second is training. Since the average tenure of the U.S. employee is approximately six years (versus 19 for Germany and eight for Britain), the return on investment for an organization's training and educational expense is not great. In an effort to restrain costs, training and development costs are continuing to be slashed. Consequently, employees are less willing to be loyal to a company that will not invest in the training and development of its staff.

Third is the rise in independent contractors, consultants, and automation. As people continue to be more expensive to employ (rise in benefit costs, workers compensation, liability insurance, government regulations, legal issues, etc.), employers are searching for broader options in their hiring practices. Employers would rather hire contractors and consultants during peak work periods and have greater flexibility to terminate consultants and contractors during the down periods. Organizations also search for options to utilize automation and computerization to reduce the dramatic increase in employee costs – sadly, employees are pricing themselves out of the marketplace given a rising litigious culture and taxes/regulations.

Fourth is the drop in full-time employment. In 2000, 56 percent of those aged 18-30 had a full time job. Today, it is less than 50 percent. Almost two thirds of the jobs created in recent months were temporary jobs, accounting for nearly 18 percent of all employment. The part-time positions pay less per hour than full-time work and also typically do not provide benefits.

The world is changing and with it so is the very nature of the workplace and society. The lesson is to learn from these changes and to better prepare yourself to excel in this different type of world.

MAKE IT ON YOUR OWN

A preeminent issue of our day is the lack of solid middle class jobs, mainly because of global competition and outsourcing. There are three reasons for this damaging event: first, there is very little difference in quality between a product made in another country and one made in the United States. Second, it costs significantly more to produce a product or service in the United States than in some foreign countries such as China, India, Vietnam, the Czech Republic, etc. Third, the United States consumer does not seem to mind or care that they are purchasing a product from another country.

The term, "Made in America" does not inspire the consumer to choose an American-made product over a foreign-produced product. If quality is similar, then it becomes an issue of price. And, if the American consumer can purchase a similar quality product from a foreign manufacturer, they will do so over an American-produced product. The stark reality is that if you are an American business-owner, or an American employee, these are difficult times for you.

You need to be competitive as a business versus foreign-owned businesses, which means you have to constantly lower your costs, because U.S. costs are much higher than foreign costs (these include social security, health care, unemployment insurance, workers compensation, insurance, etc., though many of these benefits are highly prized). Add in the rising taxes and government regulations, and the sad reality is that the American employee is more expensive to hire than foreign employees. We have seen a hollowing out of the manufacturing sector, and job opportunities are certainly less plentiful. To be competitive against a foreign-owned business, you need to produce more if you have higher prices, or lower your prices. In our case, we cannot do either, so jobs move overseas.

If you are in a job that you like, recognize that you may not be there for long. Jobs and industries change at will; the days of being in a job for 10, even five years, are becoming more the exception rather than the rule. So you need to continually upgrade your skills; there may come a time where you need to strike out on your own. You need to open your own business and sell your own product or service. Job security today is dependent on someone coming up with an idea that is new and innovative, and that no one else has thought of, and then figure out a way to sell that idea. To wait for a business to provide you a payroll check, and hoping that they do so on a continual basis, is nothing more than hope.

Take control of your future and determine your own destiny, because here is very little security in expecting a business or a government to do so. Recognize that your future is dependent more on you than someone else. You are going to have to make it on your own to have any sense of security in your future, and the earlier you recognize that fact (though it is scary and destabilizing), the more you can prepare for that future and be more confident in taking advantage of that future.

THE PURPOSE OF EDUCATION

Research indicates that – on average – the single greatest predictor of success is the number of years of education one accumulates. Consider these statistics: 35 million children, in public grammar schools, 15 million in public high schools, and 5 million in private schools. There are almost 14,000 school districts and another 31,000 private schools with over 3 million public school teachers and 400,000 private school teachers. Then there are another 21 million students attending college. Yet it amazes me how few teachers and students truly understand the meaning, value, importance and role that education plays in one's professional career and personal fulfilment.

There are many definitions of education that one can offer, some better than others. This is the one I have developed: "the basic <u>purpose</u> of education is to develop an individual's knowledge and skills so that they can **participate** in society. The hope of education, though, is more idealistic. It is that through the educational experience, one will realize their responsibility to **not only participate, but to contribute** their unique talents and gifts to the betterment of others."

The great Dr. Martin Luther King, Jr., believed that education should allow you to do three things: live well, think wisely, and act sensibly. Those that live well recognize the importance of sound mental and physical health. Those that think well can make wise and reasoned decisions. And, those that act sensibly have a sense of propriety, good manners, class and dignity. Self-esteem, confidence, and a sense of self-control are yet other attributes of those who have attained a level of education in their life, a reason the educated can involve themselves in a variety of circumstances and can adapt to the changing mores and times of which we live.

Education is the mechanism that makes you a better person, and in society it provides a better place to live. The primary deliverable, or skill, that one learns through education is the ability to become a more moral, spiritual, intellectual, and philosophical person, who can then use this knowledge to make the right decisions. This is paramount in any discussion.

THE IMPORTANCE OF KNOWLEDGE

Besides one's family, the acquisition and utilization of knowledge plays the central role in a person's development through life. The right knowledge will lead one in the right direction. It is often said that those who have gained the right knowledge are moving towards enlightenment, they are creating an enlightened soul within themselves. But it is not an easy task.

To become an enlightened soul, one needs to surround themselves with knowledge that emphasizes honesty, commitment, fidelity, and responsibility. True knowledge relates to how an individual can move their life from its current state to one where others are more important than themselves, where service is the highlight of what you do, and giving back becomes the hallmark of an enlightened life. This is one reason that knowledge is often gained through learning, and learning is the purview of a teacher.

Education is intended to provide an individual with the necessary foundation to make a better life. Being presented with interesting and thought-provoking knowledge about oneself and one's world allows one to determine their place in its future. Where does one see themselves next year, or in five years, or in 50 years? By gaining this knowledge, one can then better direct their life towards that direction.

Knowledge serves as the core principle of one's life; without knowledge as a basis, you have very little to rely upon in order to make the right decision. Learning is the process to get there. What is most interesting is that one accepts that a doctor should go to medical school to learn the art of medicine, or that a lawyer should go to law school to learn the law, or that an electrician should learn their trade from a journeyman, yet too few believe that one should read about philosophy, or logic, or literature in order to learn how to lead a better life. This knowledge, and this learning once gained, is the true light to follow in order to live the dream of dreams and gain the life that is possible.

THE CASE FOR LIBERAL EDUCATION

The word education means to "bring out or lead out" and is defined as "bringing out or leading out our capacity for life." No book on education may have had broader influence than Baldassare Castiglione's *The Courtier* (1528). This treatise sought to train, discipline, and fashion the young man into the courtly ideal, the gentleman. According to Castiglione, the educated man of the upper class should have a broad background in many academic subjects, and his spiritual and physical, as well as intellectual capabilities should be trained. The courtier should have easy familiarity with dance, music and the arts. Castiglione envisioned a man who could compose a sonnet, wrestle, sing a song and accompany himself on an instrument, ride expertly, solve difficult mathematical problems, and above all speak and write eloquently.

The Courtier largely defined and expanded upon the ideals of a liberal education. Its intention was to create a full human being, an individual blessed with character, intellect and individual style. At its very best, a liberal education is the way of life that helps make a whole human being, toward which college provides only a beginning. In four years, the student should hope to achieve a measure of that intellectual independence and creativity that is his ultimate goal. A good program of liberal education fed the student's love of truth and passion to live a good life; it flourished when it prepared the way for the discussion of a unified view of nature and man's place in it, which the best minds debated on the highest level.

True liberal education requires that the student's whole life be radically changed by it, that what he learns may affect his actions, his tastes, his choices, and that no previous attachment be immune to examination and hence re-evaluation. Similarly, a university should be the community's fountain of youth and allow a student to question what he is told and what he reads. Students should demand the basis upon which experts or authorities have reached a conclusion. He should doubt his own teachers. He should be exposed or re-exposed to as wide a variety of experiences and contrasts as possible. Above all, he should learn to search for and develop his own potential, his own individuality.

Socrates' basic philosophy was the doctrine that virtue is knowledge, or that the good life is the life of wisdom. To gain knowledge and hence virtue, he believed, education is necessary. It truly is the foundation of any moral and intellectually advanced society.

YOU GOTTA MAKE SOMETHING

Rarely do you read a newspaper or a magazine, or watch a newscast, and not hear some comment about the globalization of our world, and specifically, the outsourcing of American jobs. Some may believe that the United States is not as competitive as it used to be, and there may be some truth to that. We see that in previous recessions, there has not been a tremendous increase in jobs following the business lull. Instead, businesses have figured out how to produce or service more without adding to their payrolls. How did they do that? Mainly because they used technology to simplify the process, or they outsourced some component of production to lower-wage countries.

If you were to look around your desk, or in any store, you would be amazed how many things are made outside this country. Many of these goods were once produced by the U.S., but not anymore. We have, in so many ways, priced ourselves out of the market. Our wages in the U.S. are much higher than many or most foreign countries (think China, Korea, Vietnam, India, and many of the countries in Eastern Europe) and the benefits in those countries are virtually non-existent. Health care, unemployment insurance, workers compensation, and Medicare are not expenses that producers have to pay in many of these foreign countries. Moreover, there is not the onslaught of regulations from local, state and the federal governments that raise the prices of production. It seems the U.S. is willing to give up jobs for these social and environmental benefits and other countries are not – the end result is fewer middle class jobs today that pay a decent wage and benefits.

The simple truth is that our country does not make many things anymore because it is cheaper to make a product outside the U.S. This is not unethical or unfair, but rather necessary for survival. If U.S. businesses do not take advantage of these lower rates overseas, other firms will; those firms would then compete against higher priced U.S. goods, and the U.S. business would fail anyway. So, we will continue to see industries, and their jobs, go overseas which will cause even more havoc to our country in the coming years.

How do we fix it? Great question, but it starts with a superbly educated citizenry and the ability to produce more in the U.S. at a competitive price, and the willingness of the various governments to help maintain high quality, high paying jobs in the U.S.

GOOD AND EVIL

One search that has consumed our times is the battle between good and evil. How do you determine what is good, and what guidelines or barometers would you utilize to assess whether a thought or action that is done is good or evil? Though some struggle with the answer to that most important question, the answer may be quite simple: what is good is that which improves the human condition.

Whether someone is good or evil can be a greater challenge because we all want to be good, regardless of our own faults. Even when we lie, cheat or steal, we like to think we do so only because we are making someone else feel better or, conversely, the individual or organization had it coming. If we lie about someone else, our rationale is that they deserved it because of the way they treated us. If we steal from our organization, we rationalize it based on our belief that the organization overcharges for their product or service. We want to be seen as good because it raises our self-esteem and confidence, no matter the actions we undertake to jeopardize that basic goodness.

In contrast, evil is someone whose actions benefit largely themselves, who only have an interest in their own future. They are very difficult people to interact with because the consequences of your relationship with them will rarely benefit you, and often causes you bitterness, regret, and sadness. This is one reason I implore you to eliminate any negativity or evil from your life. It is the rare consequence where evil will lead you to become a better person or live a better life. Even if it is temporary, those with any type of conscious will soon regret their temporary act of evil and regret their actions. Those who steal from others may justify it in the short-term, but realize their profound mistake in the longer term. Unfortunately, at that time there may be nothing they can do to right the wrong that they have committed.

Pursue good in your life, and purge evil. Always look for the good along the way, no matter how much bad you may encounter. No matter the path you take, if you do so it will surely be the right road.

PONDER

At the end of the day, many dream of success but few dream of how to achieve success. Rare is the person who has spent time pondering and developing a list of traits, attributes or characteristics that would make them successful. Then, to write those down, to publish them, and then to make sure each and every thought and action of their day is directed towards developing those traits and attributes is even more rare. Only when you have a clear sense of where you are going, and have written down goals to get there, can you have the chance to reach your ambition.

Seldom does one drive from California to Idaho without referencing a map, or asking for directions. We should do the same in our personal and professional lives; obtain the necessary guidance on who you are, who you want to be, and then how you want to get there. Then, throughout your life, ensure your conduct is directed towards achieving that ambition.

It is rare for a person to develop their own mission statement or philosophy of life; those that do more often have a sense of peace, serenity, confidence and destiny in their future. Then you must get there, to develop courage, or guts, to work towards achieving your ambitions. Dreams are great, but they will never be achieved unless you work to achieve them.

So, I encourage everyone to review their life, ponder who they are and who they want to be, search out people who have succeeded in life and also appear happy and peaceful. Find out their secret of life and success, and then develop your own. Once you do, write it down and make sure every thought and action is consistent with the type of person you want to become, and the type of success you want to achieve. Then, spend your time achieving that dream. If you can do so, you will develop a sense of excitement and peace in the life you lead that only a few decent and honorable people have realized.

GREED, SELFISHNESS AND ENVY

The damage that greed, selfishness and envy can do to a person and a society is almost incalculable. Greed is the intense desire for more – there never seems to be enough. Selfishness is best represented in the thought "what's in it for me," or "take care of number 1," while envy represents the desire that "I want what you have."

No matter the type of government or economic system, there is the inevitable segmentation into the "haves" and the "have-nots." Many claim the "haves" are greedy and selfish while others claim the "have-nots" are paralyzed by envy. Both of these connotations are simply wrong. Few actually spend time or effort researching how the "haves" acquired their rewards. They often overlook the time, money, and effort that the "haves" invested in their future in the hopes of achieving the rewards. There are exceptions, of course, but few become successful without hard work, risk, and sacrifice.

Similarly, there are fewer "have-nots" that are envious of those who have succeeded, but rather believe the game is stacked against them. No matter their time, effort, or sacrifice, the end has been predetermined, and it is against their favor. They have been taught, and some come to believe, that our economic system (capitalism) is a zero-sum game—that the pie never gets bigger; thus, the person who gets a larger slice of the pie must necessarily mean others receive a smaller slice.

In reality, it is not capitalism that causes society to segment into the "haves" and "have-nots." It is a person's work ethic, courage to take a risk, and their will to sacrifice that best determines whether someone falls within the "haves" or the "have-nots." Capitalism does not cause one to prosper and another to falter; indeed, capitalism is the vehicle that allows some to attain their dreams and ambitions, if only they choose to dedicate their life to doing so. That ambition and singular drive should not be envied. In fact, it should be applauded, as its rewards are within the reach of every American.

ZEROLAND

Ethics is about the standard of right and wrong conduct, about doing the right thing. By "right," we mean that which improves our world, which makes the world a better place to be. Two pillars of ethical decision making are rationalize/justify, and a concept called "zeroland." Let's first discuss rationalization and justification.

Once a decision is made, there are often comments such as "well, there were no good choices," or "I did it for my children." These are statements made to rationalize and justify a poor decision, even a selfish decision. Rarely is there a need to rationalize and justify a decision when it is the right decision; it is only when the decision is ethically challenged that one feels the need to rationalize and justify their decision.

The second concept is called "zeroland." Most would not tell a lie for $1, or $100, or even for $1,000. But at $10,000 or $100,000? Why is it inconceivable to tell a lie for $1, but at $10,000 the question first arises, "well, what kind of lie are we talking about? Would I get caught? Who would be injured?"

The lie, or ethical misconduct, does not change if one is offered $1 versus $10,000. In reality, one's character and principles should not change no matter the money offered to do otherwise. The amount of "zeros" involved should never alter your stance; your character and principles are not "for sale" to the highest bidder. One should always do what is right no matter the repercussions involved.

Importantly, making the right ethical decisions becomes much easier when you have options. If you have saved money you are not tempted to betray your principles for a sum of money; if you can easily find another job you may not be tempted to betray your character for a promotion; if you have other friends, you are not tempted to lie and steal to maintain their friendship. The crucial lesson is to develop as many options in life as possible so that when a challenging ethical dilemma arises, it does not become a dilemma or consideration because your life has so many other possibilities. You will not, in essence, have to debate whether taking a stand on an ethical issue will result in your losing your savings, your job, or losing your friends.

JEALOUSLY AND ENVY

I hope, as we progress through life, that we become a more enlightened individual. We should learn the traits that make a person successful as well as liked and admired. Two of those traits to avoid or overcome are jealousy and envy, so I would like to spend a few minutes on becoming a better employee and person by overcoming any feelings of jealousy and envy.

To be sure, life is not easy. We look at those who are successful, wealthy, etc., and we may become jealous and envious. Some say, "that person does not deserve it," or "why do they make so much more than I do." I think, if you spend the time in an honest evaluation of what someone has to do and give up to be successful, you realize that they deserve much of what they receive; you will also realize why so many are not willing to give up much of their life to encounter the type of success that others have.

There are several reasons why you should not be jealous or envious of others who you may feel have more than you. First, if you find research on what makes a person successful, you will realize they have obtained a greater number of years of schooling. Doctors, lawyers, etc., are those who spend 20-25 years in school, a tremendous sacrifice. Second, you will find that successful people work long hours. I know few successful individuals who work eight hours a day; most work 10 hours a day, not including hours spent on work once they get home. Think of someone who owns a business and is contacted repeatedly outside their normal work hours for a decision on an important issue. Third, they have less time to spend on recreation, friends and family. When your work life consumes a greater portion of your day, you simply do not have time for many of the pleasures of life such as friends and family.

There are few successful people who become successful through luck, who did not go to school or devote a considerable period of time to their work. There usually is a cost and I do not think people realize, or accept, the cost. They see the results (the house, the car, etc.) but not what it took, or what someone had to give up, to acquire that lifestyle. I am convinced that if you told someone what they had to give up in order to have that lifestyle, many would rather not make the sacrifice.

So, as you plan your future and hope for a successful life, remember that it takes time, effort, and sacrifice. Those who are willing to do so can realize a tremendous lifestyle; those who are not willing to do so can also have a great life, but more likely one without the material successes of those who do. It is a choice, and we should not be jealous or envious of those who choose a different path for their life. Being jealous or envious of someone else is a terrible place to be because it deflects pride and accomplishment in ourselves. Concentrate on your own successes, your own life, and you will develop a sense of peace and happiness that will fulfill your heart and mind.

THE GUARANTEE

How often have we heard someone state that they did everything right, but everything turned out so wrong? That they were nice to others, studied hard in school, worked hard at their job, and contributed to society yet success and security they longed for eluded them. Such is the times that we live.

Today, we see those who devote 10 to 20 years to a company only to have their job outsourced to India or China. We see those who spend three years at night school to obtain that bachelor's or master's degree yet receive no additional compensation or promotion in the workplace (contrary to earlier promises). We see those who befriend others at the workplace or in their personal life yet soon confront the harsh realities that they were misled or misinformed as to the true nature of the friendship. Marriages start and end, jobs are created and terminated, and money earned and lost. Other than the sun rising and falling, and death and taxes, we are left with few certainties or guarantees in our future (no matter our effort or desire).

We may have little control over the events of our time, whether it is 9/11, Hurricane Katrina, or the gaining momentum of outsourcing. Events seem beyond our control as no amount of effort and desire can compensate one for being in the wrong place, at the wrong time, or for the wrong reasons. All is not lost, though, and the story is not that dire. When you study to gain as much education as possible, you are expanding your possibilities in the future. When you work to learn as much as possible in your job and industry, you create prospects for promotions and new careers. And, most importantly, when you dedicate yourself to becoming a more decent and honorable person, you unlock opportunities to meet others of a similar character and disposition.

So, while there are no guarantees that your hard work and devotion will result in a more promising tomorrow, effort is seldom wasted for one simple reason: as you work to better yourself, you think well of yourself. If you think well of yourself, you will think well of others. And if you think well of others, your jealousy and self-interest are no longer part of your character. You will find that sooner rather than later, you realize that life is what you make it; that good comes to those who invest in themselves and others. You become, more likely than not, more tolerant and accepting of your fate because you know you have done the best you could, that you could not have accomplished more. And while little is guaranteed in life, what is guaranteed is that you can make the most of what you have and place yourself in a position to take advantage of that which comes along. That, in reality, is the greatest guarantee anyone could wish for.

THE RICH

Some believe money can solve almost any problem, but sadly the solution never lasts. Money can be a reconciling influence, harmonizing conflicting forces -- but from the outside, rather than from within the individual. For those that have more money, Andrew Carnegie believed the rich should live modestly, provide moderately for their heirs and give the rest away to leave their brethren "better than they would or could do for themselves." Before he died in 1919, his benefactions totaled some $311 million, or 90% of his fortune. He donated $56 million for the construction of 2,509 libraries. The rest went mostly to colleges, special foundations and endowments and for construction in The Hague of a "Temple of Peace," now the seat of the World Court.

The question often asked is why are there such strong feelings by some with limited money against those with money? It is impossible to see any objective harm done to the less wealthy by another's greater wealth. It is not, after all, the case that the richer man's income is extracted from the poorer man. Vacationing at the shore, I see a large yacht at anchor in the harbor. Though I may wish I had one, it is quite clear that I do not lack a yacht because another man has one. The economy is not a zero/sum game – one person's gain is rarely another person's loss.

There are three types of people: the less prosperous, who are less able and/ or less successful; the equals, those most similar to our ambitions and successes; and the more prosperous, superiors, who are always just one step ahead of us. Contrary to some in politics and the media, the latter does not constitute a critical moral problem. They may be more educated, more hard working, and more fortunate, but we live in a country where you still can become that which you aspire to become if only you want to work for it, sacrifice for it, and forsake nearly everything to get it.

Life is fairer than we believe – most get what they deserve, whether it is emotionally, physically, socially or financially. It is a matter of if you want to work for it and what you are willing to give up to get it.

PASS AND REPASS

When my grandmother was a young mother, her husband left her for another woman. Though she had every reason to be resentful, she told herself to "pass and repass." My mother, then, was not only raised without a father who was around every day but without one who financially supported her at all—no alimony, no child support. This was many years ago when few opportunities were available to women, so my grandmother and her family relied on welfare to provide the basic necessities of life.

More difficult for my mom, though, was the absence of any cards or gifts from her father during her youth and the ridicule from her classmates because she wore shoes that did not match and clothes that did not fit. Though she had every reason to be bitter, she learned the invaluable saying, "pass and repass," that life is a continual transition from one state or circumstance to another. What happens today will most likely not happen tomorrow. It means that "this too shall pass."

More importantly, "pass and repass" is a reminder that you will experience periods of profound anger and loss in this life. These experiences are often the result of what is done to you by other people, but you do have a choice: you can become bitter and resentful, or you can remember to "pass and repass." Let go of that which is hurtful to you; be reminded that although others have aggrieved you—often by intention and with malice—you will persevere and become an even better person. You have "passed" through the worst that life has to offer and have "repassed" through those who take satisfaction only in tearing others down.

On his last day in office, President Nixon said, "Others may hate you, but they do not win until you hate them back, and then you destroy yourself." It is a lesson to remember to never let others affect your future, your life. Ensure that when those with malicious intentions create obstacles to your happiness, you "pass and repass" through the best and worst that life has to offer. You can then overcome any difficulty with courage and with the hope that those who inflict such damage on others find – at some point in their lives – the peace that comes with doing the best and thinking the best of those you encounter in your life. They have to live that life, but you surely do not.

PRICE WE PAY

Fame and fortune, respect and prominence, attest to a life of significance, to a person of importance. But there is nearly always a price to pay as one pursues greatness – the journey demands considerable sacrifice, an all-encompassing focus, and incredibly long hours. Those who aspire for greatness become well aware of the sacrifices that need to be made: time away from home, the stress and anxiety from a highly responsible position, and often the envy and jealousy of colleagues and subordinates. Working hard—even at something you like—requires a sacrifice many are only too willing to make in the beginning, but their enthusiasm for their dream diminishes as the sacrifices required to achieve it escalate. It is an incredible price to pay and a tremendous sacrifice to bear. Few people are willing to pay that price.

Fortunately, there are those solitary few who are willing to pay any price and bear any burden to achieve greatness. These few spend their waking hours not only perfecting their unique gifts and talents, but then they do something with them. Many do not rest on their laurels, or accomplishments, or the knowledge that they have gained. Few take their gifts and talents "for a spin" and work to employ a community, feed the hungry, help the aged, and teach children to read.

No matter the gift or talent, over time those who achieve a sense of pride and meaning are those who have used some of their gifts and talents, or what they have achieved through their gifts and talents, to the benefit of others. The price to be paid for success in life is worthwhile when you can do something – anything – for those less fortunate. It is an act of unselfishness that, as you progress through life, gives you the greatest satisfaction, regardless and in place of whatever wealth or fame you may achieve on a personal level.

The great sacrifice takes much to achieve success, and there is a heady price to pay along that road. Yet sacrifices in the pursuit of something decent and honorable can make for an exhilarating, exciting experience, one that may define your life. Those who avoid the sacrifices that are required in the pursuit of their ambitions end their lives as a dreamer of dreams, rather than a doer of deeds. That is a terrible tragedy. Do something with what you have; become someone better than you are. It may be a challenge for the ages, but it is a worth price to pay in your journey to greatness.

PEOPLE

We often hear comments like, "our people are our greatest resource," or "the employee drives the innovation of a company." These are statements heard fairly often in the business world. Are they true? I believe it is becoming less and less true. Here is why: the right person is the most important asset of a business. That person with unique and innovative skills, who offers a mental or physical ability that is above and beyond the capabilities of most employees in my opinion, is called a 'superstar' and the success and failure of a business will revolve around the success of that person. But, unfortunately, there are very few people who are in an organization that can make that type of change, and therefore the overall strength or capabilities of a firm are less than desired.

An organization wants those one or two individuals whose mind is so advanced, so innovative, so progressive, that they literally drag an organization to greatness. It is that leader, or manager, or employee, who thinks differently, who is able to create a market that the organization can then fill. An example would be a sales representative who dreams of an innovative manner in which to sell a product, or the pioneering marketing director who creates a product that will then dominate the market. These individuals are not just superstars, but 'game changers.' They change the very direction not only of the organization, but the marketplace as well.

Organizations that can hire, retain and promote these individuals are the organizations that will reach the upper echelons of their industry. It is those one or two individuals that offer this promise, and it is those one or two individuals that an organization should concentrate on and promote. While it is true that you need a wide array of people to make an organization work, I believe those skills are fairly common; what is uncommon is those skills and abilities to dream, to create, and to envision a product or service that has yet to be developed and will dominate the competitive landscape once it is developed. It is these uncommon individuals who are receiving the uncommon (high) incomes, and is the principle reason for the income disparity between individuals. Become an uncommon employee and you will not only secure your future employment, but will secure your financial independence as well.

EDUCATION AND EXPERIENCE

In an unstable, contentious, and often traumatic world, the ability to influence events offers a better chance to control the future. Influence is achieved through a variety of mechanisms, with education and experience among the most prevalent. Through education we are exposed to and become influenced by the great thoughts and words of history. This accumulated knowledge makes us a more moral, spiritual, philosophical and enlightened person, who can then use this knowledge to make the right decision at the right time and for the right reasons. Reasoned and rational decisions can be made, one where selfish or self-interested ambitions are thwarted and a more balanced and fair approach is achieved.

Conversely, the influence through experience is more complex. Experience relies upon one's own history, not the accumulated histories of others. One's experience is typically sheltered and solitary – our experiences are limited by our own journey. Experience without adolescence, college, marriage, children, a career, financial stresses, health concerns, and older age can be narrow and biased, betraying the knowledge necessary to make informed and deliberate decisions. Without the richness of a full and broad life one becomes a baseball player trying to hit without a bat, or a tennis player serving without a racket. Those relying on experience must, then, live a full and complex life composed of terrifying highs and unbelievable lows, all of which frame our perspective about life and our place in it.

The greater and more varied the experiences, the better chance one can make the right decision, or at least a better decision. With a solid educational foundation to rest upon – one that provides the theories, concepts, strategies, perspectives, and histories – and the wise experiences that come from living a rich and meaningful life, a more studied and considered decision can be made, and a better and more consequential life can be led.

THE PLATFORM

No matter one's station in life – their heritage, education, or talent – there lies within each person something unique, even odd, that stands as their distinguishing characteristics in society. That unique characteristic – a trait foreign to most others – can serve as their platform to greatness, if they only choose to use it.

A platform is something that you are good at, something that others will pay to see, something that makes you more different or unique than other people. That platform elevates you versus your competitors, co-workers, and friends. In that area and on that platform, you are the star: an actor has a platform in the theater classroom, a teacher has a platform in the classroom a doctor has a platform in the Emergency Room, and a parent has a platform in their home with their children.

This platform gives you an opportunity to educate, to provide some entertainment or amusement to others, and to provide a knowledge or skill to someone else that they cannot do themselves. The truly sad aspect is that most people do not use the platform that they have been given to its fullest extent. If painting is their platform, some would not pursue that venture because the financial rewards may not be sufficient. If teaching is their platform, some may not pursue teaching because of the lack of long-term growth. They have a platform, which they may not choose to use.

Every person is given a platform: a teacher, a singer, a carpenter. What you do with that platform determines the pride in your past, the happiness in your present, and the legacy for your future. The hope for everyone is that they know what their platform is, and then do something to use that platform for the benefit of others. If all the world's inhabitants utilized their platform to its fullest potential, we would witness a truly remarkable view: the best paintings, the best teachers, the best doctors, the best lawyers, all directed towards achieving their potential and allowing the rest of us to view in awe their unique gifts and potentials.

My hope is that you follow your potential, and your platform, to illuminate the world to a better place.

LOOKING BACK

In general, we learn from the past, then work to make a better future. I am convinced, though, that as the years progress we tend to spend more time looking back (over memories, achievements, lost opportunities, etc.), than looking forward. This may arise because at a certain point we have more time that has passed than is in front of us. (Someone once said if you can double your age and have a reasonable chance of getting there, you are still on the upswing!)

As we do travel through life, then, it becomes even more important that as we look back we are consumed with pride and a sincere sense of accomplishment over what we have done. Never say time ran out; be able to say you used every second of time you were granted. Never say you lacked talent or the ability to win; be able to say you used all you were granted and left everything on the field. And, never say you were afraid of failure; be able to say you had the courage to try. This is the mark of someone who can look back, as the years progress, on a life that had purpose, on a life that has been lived, and on a life that made a difference.

TALENT AND SUPERSTARS

Next to hard work, talent is the most important characteristic of a successful person. Most organizations have the same access to capital, equipment, etc., but they do not have the same access to talent, those people who are often called "superstars." Today, it is not the stars of an organization that give it its competitive advantage but those very few people who have a knowledge, skill, or ability that is unique to their industry, or even their world. It is those people who possess a sense of greatness that is distinct and exceptional, two traits that define who they are and belie their importance.

These "superstars" are the dominant force in their field who determine the innovative approaches to not only solving the problems of the day, but also are instrumental in dreaming up the catalytic events that will shape the future. Think of any successful company of the day and you will most likely encounter a few individuals who have shaped the destiny of that firm. They are the builders and dreamers, the ones who transformed what could be, to what will be, to what is. It is these superstars that the organization must search for and ensure never leave the organization.

The oratorical eloquence of Ronald Reagan, the musical ear of singer Michael W. Smith, and deft hand-eye coordination of tennis player Roger Federer may be talents that originate from their birth. Rarely, however, are gifts given that are in such abundance and are so complete that no training or practice is required to perfect that gift. Talent, yes, one must also work hard to perfect it. It is the combination of drive and determination, along with sacrifice, that separates the common, average person from the uncommon, great person manager.

For while many like to say it is the "people" who are the source of success, it is in reality those very few superstars that control the future. Find them, or be one, and your fate is secure.

GOTTA HAVE A LITTLE LUCK

No matter how hard you work, or how stridently you go down swinging for what you believe in, there is some truth in the saying that you "gotta have a little luck." A few people are born wealthy or naturally beautiful. There is little they did to realize their fate, so they are lucky. But I am convinced that everyone has some "luck" in their life, whether it be the way they look, the build of their body, the ambitions in their heart, and intelligence in their mind. There is a mistaken tendency to believe that if someone is lucky in one area of their life (fame, fortune, etc.) then they are lucky in all areas of their life. If you study the lives of the rich and famous, you soon realize this is far from the truth.

What is true is that, for the most part, you put yourself in a position where luck can present itself. For example, there is the person who just received a great promotion, and the implication from some is they were lucky or they were there at the right time. Too many remember that the person spent years acquiring the education that few others that applied had, that they worked harder and had more successes, or that they spent more time preparing and practicing for the interview. Of course, the individual was fortunate, even lucky, that the position became vacant, but they also had to put themselves in a position to take advantage of that opportunity.

Here is another example: you save your money and invest in a business, and fortune arises that the economy is growing and customers have more disposable income. Through hard work and sacrifice, over time you finally realize some financial security. Based on your new-found wealth, some are led to believe you were lucky, forgetting the risk you took, the sacrifice you endured, neglected your family and friends for long periods of time, and the exorbitant hours you worked in the hopes of realizing your dream. They often look at the end result (wealth) rather than the means (risk, sacrifice, long hours, etc.) as they sit in judgment, when in reality if they looked at the means first, they would believe that the ends were fair and justified.

Luck is not the controlling factor in your future, but it can be a factor in your success, but only when you work hard to place yourself in a position where – once luck presents itself – you are able to take advantage of it.

WHAT YOU DID WITH WHAT YOU HAD

I have long believed that, at the end of your life, you will be asked some variation of "what did you do with what you had?" For those born into money, the question may be, "what did you do with the money you were given." Others were born with incredible athletic skills, the question may be "what did you do with all that once-in-a-generation talent? And there are others whose intellectual skills defy logic and will be asked, "with that unbelievable mind, what did you do with it? At some point, you will be asked what you did with the talents, abilities, advantages, strengths and luck that you – and only you – were granted at some point in your life.

Just as good fortune enters life unexpectedly, so too does disaster and heartache. Those blessed with a long life inevitably encounter – at some point – illness, divorce, financial losses, lack of gainful employment, or personal traumas. It is the rare person who leaves this Earth unscathed by struggles, loss and regret. But tragedy and defeat rarely become the defining characteristic of a life for those determined to bear any burden, and persevere through any struggle, to achieve their noble ambitions during their years on Earth.

Live your life so that you have made the most out of everything you were given, that you persevered over those illnesses and financial setbacks to make the most of your life, that you dedicated your life to make the most of your physical talents and mental abilities. That, when the game we call life nears its end, we can humbly and honestly say that, "we did the best we could with everything we were given," that we reached our potential, and that we contributed to the betterment of mankind.

THE ROAD TO GOOD

Negativity, often described as being a negative person or being in a negative environment, has a profound impact on a person's mind, actions and behavior. I once read, "associate not with evil lest you increase their numbers." What that means is that you associate yourself with negative people, people who do the wrong things for the wrong reasons, eventually you will become that type of person too.

It is quite difficult, though, to develop and maintain a positive attitude. We are so conditioned to believe that if we encounter red lights as we go to work, or if our car breaks down, or if there is a bad circumstance at work, that our whole day or whole week is doomed. Frankly, though, there is so much more that can happen to you that is good rather than bad. For instance, you can actually get up after a night's sleep; a great majority of us can see, and walk, and have people in our lives that make every day special (whether that be a spouse, a child, or a friend). It is unfortunate, really, that so many concentrate on the negative.

How do you learn to concentrate on the positive, on the good? I would add that it is incredibly difficult. I often believe that it is nearly impossible to focus on the good when, for too long, you have pondered the negative. It takes one who truly wants to change their persona, their personality, and their outlook. This is done by keeping foremost in your mind the belief that you should always look for the good. When others put you down (which is so common), when others believe you simply cannot make it, when others think that it cannot be done, you have to believe that it can. You have to believe that goodness will always triumph over evil, and that those who are "bad" in their beliefs and opinions really do a disservice to themselves, rather than doing a disservice to you.

It is tough, but not impossible. Looking to the good means that you wonder at the great weather of the day, appreciate the people who you interact with throughout the course of your travels (even if they do not appreciate you), and that you are grateful for the good fortune that you have, even if some may claim your good fortune is less than they have. It means that you always look to the good and always appreciate what you have. These are the hallmarks of those who live a life that, in the end, others envy and can only admire from their life of negativity and regret. More than anything, always look to the good along the road of life.

THE SYSTEM

Most are raised to respect their elders, follow the "rules," and be a "team" player. It is inherently contrary to our upbringing to challenge authority; we are taught to work within the "system" in order to be accepted and get ahead. Yet innovative strategies and substantive change arise from challenging the very system one was taught to respect and uphold.

When is the right time to fight authority and the "system?" There are times when it is appropriate and even encouraged to "not be a team player" and work collaboratively yet forcefully to fight the system, to raise the awareness of perilous impediments to a better future for all, not simply the few. There are times when rules should not stop you from thinking or acting merely because a rule says you should, and seldom let a policy dictate you should do or should not do something because "that is the way it has always worked." Question the relevance and appropriateness of what you see and hear to ensure it is right and just, and you may find that as you do others may enter the fray to support your intentions.

There are too many, however, who enter the ring to fight the battle simply because they enjoy the contentious nature of argument and frustration. They are negative and maladjusted individuals who revel in conflict and divisiveness, wrongly believing the challenges of others make their own seem far less troubled. By tearing others down, they believe their own disappointments and failures are commonplace. Nothing is farther from the truth.

Conversely, there are too few of the "right" people, those who are honest and unselfish in their pursuit, who choose to fight the system. It is much easier to "go along to get along" and follow the crowd that have established the path that you now follow. It certainly takes less work and far less stress to avoid confronting those who work to benefit today from the systems and processes created yesterday. Therein lies the complex nature of changing nearly any relationship, organization or country: there are those who benefit from "the way things are" and will work forcefully to defend those benefits from anyone working to change them. That is why fighting the system is such an arduous task.

It is the unique person who "fights the system" to make something better for the right reason and at the right time. It is even more rare to find the unique person who fights to make something better when they personally have nothing to gain from the outcome, when they do not benefit from working for a higher wage, a better product, a more profitable company, or the abolition of a deceptive practice or discriminatory action. These individuals are few in number, but their impact is grander in scale, simply because they had the fortitude to fight the system.

LEGACY

Helping others. Contributing. Making the world a better place to live. As we progress through life, we think more and more about what we have done for other people, what we have done that has mattered, and what we have done to make the world better. We become consumed with our legacy, by what we will leave behind that will mark our existence.

All too often, we realize that our legacy will not involve the size of our house, the type of car we drove, the job we had, or the money we made. More often, those experiences that shape our legacy are those involving courageous actions (fighting for our country), principled stands (fighting against toxic dumps and improving the state of our nation's educational system), and moral character (honesty, wisdom, justice, and self-discipline). Think of any great person in your life and you are most likely to remember that they did what was right, at the right time, and for the right reasons. That they stood up for those who could not stand up for themselves, or for something few were willing to do because the cost to their career or financial future was too great. As someone who, no matter the price to pay or the burden to carry, was willing to do so because that defined who they were. It was their legacy.

I hope, as you determine your own legacy, you are guided by two thoughts: First, time; I became more conscious that it goes by much too quickly. Life seems to pass quickly by so many people. The precious gift of time is given to each of us without any certainty, without the promise of a tomorrow. Therefore, as the saying goes, never put off until tomorrow what you can do today.

Second, regrets; I became more familiar with people who were entering the closing stages of their lives, who had profound regrets about what little they had accomplished during their time on earth. These people said that if they could do it all over again, they would have overcome their jealousies and insecurities, and any other obstacles along their paths, and would have followed their own hearts. In doing so, they would have left as "someone of value" to their families and their communities; their time on earth would have been worthwhile; and they would have had a purpose to their lives.

Work hard at work worth doing

Section 8

THE BACKPACK

THE BACKPACK

The search to make a difference – one that defines our existence and determines our legacy – is the seminal journey of our life. It is those who want to make a difference that endure the uncertainties, challenges, and difficulties associated with great change. Through struggles and challenges, the will to make a difference, to make something better for others, overpowers the will to make something better for ourselves. A sense of pride and hope pervades those whose interests far exceed their own, and this ambition can be intoxicating for the individual who comes to believe in the power of a different, yet better, future. It is this type of person who seeks to make a difference in the lives of others.

In the dawn of life, we strive to make a living; in the twilight of life, we strive to make a difference. In our younger years, we abuse the environment for our own pleasure; in our later years, we work to save the environment for others' pleasure. As young adults, we spent more than we saved, used more than we made, and taken more than we have given. It is education, our experiences, our influences, and maturity that change our perspectives as time advances. We realize we may have made a life, but not a difference, and that disappointment and regret haunts our soul. We strive to make a difference because we realize we have not.

If only we strived to make a difference throughout the entirety of our life, rather than only at the end when the sands of time slip through the hourglass of time. What if we worked to save the environment, shelter the homeless, and feed the hungry in our younger years? What if we helped those with speech impediments to speak more fluidly or advised high school seniors on how to weather the life-altering experiences as a college freshman? Quite possibly, we could have changed the trajectory of their future rather than waiting until their fate had been determined.

This reminds me of a story I wrote some time ago called, "The Story of the Backpack." I believe that when we are born, we are given a backpack with certain traits, characteristics, talents, and advantages. We then spend the remaining moments of our life perfecting those traits, characteristics, talents, and advantages. We spend our lives trying to "do something" with what we were given in that backpack. It matters little whether we ever achieved our hopes and dreams....what matters is that we tried. We will never have global peace, feed all the world's hungry, or cure catastrophic diseases and illnesses. What matters is that we tried, that we worked to make the world a better place. What matters is that – at the end of your life – you can return the backpack and say that you did the best you could with what you had, that you fought the good fight, that you did what was right, and that – in some small way – your life made a difference in this world.

It is the reason I carry a backpack every day of my life.

In the end, we are only limited by our dreams of a better world and the determination to make a difference. We can help others to be grateful for what they have and not ungrateful for what they do not have, to give more than they take, to assume responsibility for their actions rather than seek others to blame for their own misdeeds, and to rebuild our planet rather than destroying its natural resources. We can help ourselves by always looking for the good along the road of life, go down swinging for what we believe in, and doing something – anything – with our time on Earth to contribute to the betterment of mankind. If this can be said as we enter the later stages of our life, we can say our life had true meaning, that we mattered, and that, in some small way, made a difference with our time here on Earth.

Printed in the United States
By Bookmasters